CINCO DE MAYO

BY **LINDA LOWERY**

ILLUSTRATIONS BY **BARBARA KNUTSON**

On My Own

HOLIDAYS

Carolrhoda Books, Inc./Minneapolis

This book is available in two editions:
Library binding by Carolrhoda Books, Inc., a division of Lerner Publishing Group
Soft cover by First Avenue Editions, an imprint of Lerner Publishing Group
241 First Avenue North
Minneapolis, MN 55401 U.S.A.

Website address: www.carolrhodabooks.com

Library of Congress Cataloging-in-Publication Data

Lowery, Linda.
    Cinco de mayo / by Linda Lowery ; illustrations by Barbara Knutson.
        p.   cm. — (On my own holidays)
    ISBN: 1–57505–654–2 (lib. bdg. : alk. paper)
    ISBN: 1–57505–764–6 (pbk. : alk. paper)
    1. Cinco de Mayo (Mexican holiday)—Juvenile literature. 2. Mexico—Social life and customs—Juvenile literature. 3. Cinco de Mayo, Battle of, Puebla, Mexico, 1862— Juvenile literature. I. Title: 5 de mayo. II. Knutson, Barbara. III. Title. IV. Series.
    F1233.L876 2005
    394.262—dc22   2004004461

Manufactured in the United States of America
1 2 3 4 5 6 – DP – 10 09 08 07 06 05

for Kathy Garcia, un amiga del alma
—L.L.

Piñatas packed with candy!

Fireworks!

Dancing in the streets!

¿Qué pasa?

What's going on?

It's Cinco de Mayo!

Cinco de Mayo is the fifth day of May.
It is a fiesta day in the United States
and in Mexico.
On a fiesta day, everyone celebrates.
Cinco de Mayo is when people remember
an amazing battle that took place
more than 100 years ago.

The story of Cinco de Mayo is
a story of courage.
It is a story of Mexican soldiers
who changed history by beating
the strongest army on Earth.
It is a story of the people of Mexico and
the United States, working together.

Two Presidents and an Emperor
1861

Mexico was tired of war.

For hundreds of years,

Spain had ruled Mexico.

Many Mexican people had lost their lives

fighting to get rid of the Spanish.

The Spanish left in 1821.

In the 1840s, a new war broke out

between Mexico and the United States.

Mexico lost half its land.

Now, in 1861, the Mexican people

were finally free.

They had a president who was Mexican.

He came from a tribe of Indians

called the Zapotecs.

His name was Benito Juárez.

Benito was the first Indian to become
the president of Mexico.
He had grown up poor.
He was an orphan.
He worked as a shepherd
for one of his uncles.
Benito studied hard.
He went to college and became a lawyer.

In 1861, Benito Juárez became
the president of Mexico.
He proved that even a poor shepherd
could be educated and grow up
to lead his country.
Benito hoped that Mexico and the United
States could become friends.
He began writing letters to the president
of the United States.

Abraham Lincoln was president
of the United States.
He was happy to hear from Benito Juárez.
Abe and Benito were very similar.
Abe had also been born poor.
He grew up in a log cabin.
He studied hard
and became a lawyer.
Now Abe was leading
his country, and he had
a war to deal with.
The states in the North were fighting
the states in the South.
This war was called the Civil War.
Abe Lincoln was worried.
He knew that the emperor of France
was thinking about sending soldiers
and weapons to help the South.

With this help, the South would
probably win the Civil War.
The United States would be two countries
instead of one.

The French emperor's name
was Napoleon III.
His army was the best in the whole world.
Their uniforms were brand new.
Their tall boots were shiny.
Their weapons were deadly.
Napoleon was greedy.
He wanted to rule all of Latin America.
He also wanted the South
to win the Civil War.

Then the United States would be weak.
France would be the most powerful nation
in the world.
Napoleon decided to attack
and capture Mexico.
Then he would be able to move his army
across the border to help the South.
President Abe Lincoln was worried.
President Benito Juárez was worried.
They knew that if their countries were to
remain free, they had to work together.

The Battle of Puebla

Ships full of French soldiers came sailing
across the Atlantic Ocean in late 1861.
They landed in Mexico,
at a port called Veracruz.
Napoleon III told his soldiers
to attack Mexico City.
Mexico City is the capital of Mexico.

It was the home of Benito Juárez
and his government.

On the way, the French soldiers stopped
in villages to eat and sleep.

The Mexican people were afraid
of the French soldiers.

There was very little fighting.

The French began to think that
the Mexicans were cowards.

Benito Juárez knew that his people
were not cowards.
They were simply tired of fighting.
But something had to be done.
Benito knew that Napoleon wanted to
replace him with a fancy European prince.
Then the Mexicans would not be free.
Napoleon also wanted to take Mexico's
gold and silver for France.

Worst of all, he wanted to stamp out
the Mexican way of life.
But what could Benito Juárez do?
There was no money to train soldiers.
There was no money to buy
weapons and bullets.
All Benito could do was to send a small
army to try to stop the French.
The two armies would meet in Puebla,
a town east of Mexico City.

The Mexicans had about 3,000 soldiers.

There were 6,000 French soldiers.

The Mexican army asked farmers for help.

The farmers were called campesinos.

They wore straw hats and serapes and

homemade sandals.

They had only farm tools as weapons.

But the Mexicans had

a very important strength.

Their hearts were in this war.

They were not just protecting their

treasures of gold and silver.

They were protecting their own homes

and their own families.

They were protecting their traditions.

They were protecting all the children

who would grow up Mexican.

It was May 5, 1862, el cinco de mayo.
The Mexican army knew that the French
planned to attack Puebla this very day.
At dawn, the cathedral bell rang out.
The campesinos grabbed shovels
and sharp knives called machetes.
They rushed to join the Mexican troops.
The campesinos and some of the soldiers
hid in trenches near Puebla's two forts.

In the meantime, the French army stopped
to drink their morning coffee.
There had been no trouble
in any Mexican town so far.
Why would they find trouble in Puebla?
They knew that only a miserable little
army was waiting.
This would be an easy battle.

Boldly, the French stormed the forts.
They scrambled up the stone walls
to shoot the Mexicans.
The Mexicans shot back.
Hundreds of French soldiers
tumbled down.

More French soldiers rushed up the walls.

Those soldiers were also shot.

Soon the French had used up most of

their bullets and cannonballs.

This tattered army of Mexicans

was beating them!

How was that possible?

Suddenly thunder boomed across the sky.

Lightning cracked and rain poured down.

The French horses began to slip
in the mud.

The men in the trenches leaped out
and began to shoot.

Campesinos waved their machetes
and stirred up nearby cattle.
The cattle charged the French soldiers,
who went sliding in the sloppy mud.
By late afternoon, the French
had lost the battle.
They turned around
and headed back east.

In Puebla, church bells rang all night long.
Mexican soldiers, helped by
Mexican farmers, had beaten an army
twice the size of their own.
They had beaten an army that had not lost a
battle in many years!
As soon as he got the news, Benito Juárez
made the victory a national celebration.
After Cinco de Mayo, many Mexicans saw
themselves in a new way.
"¡Yo soy Mexicano!" people cried.
"I am Mexican!"
They were proud to be Mexican.
They were not powerless against invaders.
They were determined to rule
their own country.

The Mexican people needed
that determination.
Napoleon sent 30,000 more
French soldiers to Mexico.
For three years, the Mexicans kept
battling the French.

During that time, every May fifth,
Mexicans took time to celebrate.
They proudly remembered
their victory at Puebla.
It reminded them to stay brave and fight
for their heart's desire, a free Mexico.

During those years, the Civil War
went on in the United States.

The South grew poorer and weaker.

France could not help the South.

To keep Mexico under control,
Napoleon had sent more soldiers, horses,
food, and weapons.

He had no extra money for the South.

In the meantime, President Lincoln
and President Juárez kept in touch.

As soon as he could,
Abraham Lincoln sent guns
and bullets to Mexico.

When the Civil War ended in 1865,
Lincoln rushed soldiers to the border.

Now it was Napoleon who was worried.

The United States was standing
together with Mexico.

Was Napoleon going to continue this war?

No, he decided.

Finally, in 1867, the French left Mexico.

Never again has a European army

invaded the Americas.

¡Fiesta!

Since May 5, 1862, Mexicans and
Americans have been good neighbors.
Together, they have fought for freedom
in many wars.
Every year, on both sides of the border,
we celebrate Cinco de Mayo.

The biggest celebration takes place
in Puebla, Mexico.
People get up early and head for the
Boulevard of the Heroes of Cinco de Mayo.
There, they rent chairs
to watch the parade.
It is noisy and crowded.

The sun beats down.

Merchants holler, selling cotton candy,
bubbles, and binoculars.

"¡Sombreros!" they call.

"Straw hats!"

There are paper parasols in bright colors.

Balloon sellers carry huge clouds
of balloons.

By noon, the parade begins.

Colorful floats pass by,

proudly showing the history of Mexico.

School bands play songs they have

practiced for months.

Soldiers march in straight columns.

Children dress up like campesinos.

They carry machetes and shovels.

People clap and toss confetti.

Little bits of pink, blue, green,

purple, and yellow paper

shower down on the parade.

That night there is a show
on the famous battlefield.
People dress up like soldiers
and act out the Battle of Puebla.

They do not use bullets and cannonballs.
Instead they toss flowers at each other.
They throw eggshells filled with confetti.
Fireworks burst in the sky
above Puebla's forts.

In the United States, Cinco de Mayo
has become a big fiesta too.
It was not always that way.
In the 1960s, Mexican Americans wanted
to share their culture.
They were proud of their Mexican roots.
They began celebrating Cinco de Mayo.

They invited neighbors to join in the fun.
Now cities across the United States hold
parades on the fifth of May.
Some people dress in the red, white, and
green colors of the Mexican flag.
Others wear traditional costumes from
different states of Mexico.

Families serve traditional Mexican foods.

There are tacos and enchiladas

and spicy snacks.

One of the most famous dishes,

called mole, comes from Puebla.

It is a sauce made with 40 ingredients,

including chilies and spices and chocolate.

Children burst piñatas packed
with candy, fruit, and tiny toys.
People dance to the guitars and trumpets
of mariachi players.
The day ends with fireworks,
laser light shows, and concerts.

On Cinco de Mayo,
Mexicans and Americans
celebrate together.
We celebrate the small army
that won over great odds.

We celebrate the food and history
and music of the Mexican people.
We celebrate good neighbors.
¡Viva el Cinco de Mayo!
Long live Cinco de Mayo!

Spanish Words

campesinos (KAHM-pay-SEE-nohs): farm workers

Cinco de Mayo (SEENK-oh DAY MY-oh): the fifth of May

fiesta (fee-ES-tah): a celebration or party

machetes (mah-CHEH-tays): large knives used to cut crops in the fields

mariachi (MAHR-ee-AH-chee): a type of musician who wears a traditional Mexican costume and plays fiesta music in a band

mole (MOH-lay): a spicy sauce for meats and Mexican dishes

piñatas (peen-YAH-tahs): colorful paper containers, filled with toys and candy, that children break open at fiestas

serapes (sehr-AH-pays): wool cloaks worn over the shoulders

sombreros (sohm-BREH-rohs): hats that are made of cloth or straw and often have a wide brim